AWESOME DOGS

Australian Cattle Dogs

by Lindsay Shaffer

BLASTOFF!
2
READERS

BELLWETHER MEDIA • MINNEAPOLIS, MN

Note to Librarians, Teachers, and Parents:

Blastoff! Readers are carefully developed by literacy experts and combine standards-based content with developmentally appropriate text.

Level 1 provides the most support through repetition of high-frequency words, light text, predictable sentence patterns, and strong visual support.

Level 2 offers early readers a bit more challenge through varied simple sentences, increased text load, and less repetition of high-frequency words.

Level 3 advances early-fluent readers toward fluency through increased text and concept load, less reliance on visuals, longer sentences, and more literary language.

Level 4 builds reading stamina by providing more text per page, increased use of punctuation, greater variation in sentence patterns, and increasingly challenging vocabulary.

Level 5 encourages children to move from "learning to read" to "reading to learn" by providing even more text, varied writing styles, and less familiar topics.

Whichever book is right for your reader, Blastoff! Readers are the perfect books to build confidence and encourage a love of reading that will last a lifetime!

This edition first published in 2019 by Bellwether Media, Inc.

No part of this publication may be reproduced in whole or in part without written permission of the publisher. For information regarding permission, write to Bellwether Media, Inc., Attention: Permissions Department, 6012 Blue Circle Drive, Minnetonka, MN 55343.

Library of Congress Cataloging-in-Publication Data

Names: Shaffer, Lindsay, author.
Title: Australian Cattle Dogs / by Lindsay Shaffer.
Description: Minneapolis, MN : Bellwether Media, Inc., 2019. | Series:
   Blastoff! Readers. Awesome Dogs | Audience: Age 5-8. | Audience: K to
   Grade 3. | Includes bibliographical references and index.
Identifiers: LCCN 2018032012 (print) | LCCN 2018037520 (ebook) | ISBN
   9781681036366 (ebook) | ISBN 9781626179059 (hardcover : alk. paper)
Subjects: LCSH: Australian cattle dog-Juvenile literature.
Classification: LCC SF429.A77 (ebook) | LCC SF429.A77 S53 2019 (print) | DDC 636.737-dc23
LC record available at https://lccn.loc.gov/2018032012

Text copyright © 2019 by Bellwether Media, Inc. BLASTOFF! READERS and associated logos are trademarks and/or registered trademarks of Bellwether Media, Inc. SCHOLASTIC, CHILDREN'S PRESS, and associated logos are trademarks and/or registered trademarks of Scholastic Inc., 557 Broadway, New York, NY 10012.

Editor: Betsy Rathburn   Designer: Laura Sowers

Printed in the United States of America, North Mankato, MN.

Table of Contents

What Are Australian Cattle Dogs?

Australian cattle dogs are smart and active dogs. They love to work and play.

They are also called
red or blue heelers or
Queensland heelers.

Australian cattle dogs
are strong and **stocky**.
Their powerful muscles
make them great runners.

These medium-sized dogs weigh
up to 50 pounds (23 kilograms)!

Strong Dogs with Speckled Coats

Australian cattle dogs have short **coats**. They may be red or blue with speckled markings.

Australian Cattle Dog Coats

blue   red

Outer hairs lie above a thick **undercoat**. This keeps the dogs warm and dry.

These dogs have wide heads.
Their eyes are **alert** and **curious**.

Their triangle-shaped ears
point to the sky!

History of Australian Cattle Dogs

Australian cattle dogs were **bred** in Australia in the 1800s. Farmers used them to gather herds.

Australia

Farmers bred collies and **dingoes**. Later, Dalmatians added speckles to the **breed**!

Australian Cattle Dog Profile

triangle-shaped
ears

speckled coat

stocky body

Life Span: 12 to 16 years

Trainability:

1 2 3 4 5 6

Hardest to train   Easiest to train

Australian cattle dogs joined
the **Herding Group** of the
American Kennel Club
in 1980.

Today, the dogs still work on cattle farms. They are also favorite pets!

Australian cattle dogs have a lot of energy. They love to go on walks and run in backyards.

Their **stamina** makes them great pets for hikers.

These dogs also have active minds. They can learn to herd and do tricks.

They also love to run **agility** courses!

agility course

19

Australian Cattle Dogs are **loyal** friends. They make great watchdogs.

These sweet dogs love
their human families!

Glossary

agility—a dog sport where dogs run through a series of obstacles

alert—quick to notice or act

American Kennel Club—an organization that keeps track of dog breeds in the United States

bred—purposely mated two dogs to make puppies with certain qualities

breed—a type of dog

coats—the hair or fur covering some animals

curious—interested or excited to learn or know about something

dingoes—wild dogs that live in Australia

Herding Group—a group of dog breeds that like to control the movement of other animals

loyal—having constant support for someone

stamina—the ability to exercise for a long time

stocky—having a solid, heavy body

undercoat—short, soft hair or fur that keeps some dog breeds warm

To Learn More

AT THE LIBRARY
Gagne, Tammy. *The Dog Encyclopedia for Kids.*
North Mankato, Minn.: Capstone Young Readers,
2017.

Polinsky, Paige V. *Australian Cattle Dogs.*
Minneapolis, Minn.: Abdo Publishing, 2017.

Schuh, Mari. *Collies.* Minneapolis, Minn.: Bellwether
Media, 2018.

ON THE WEB

FACTSURFER

Factsurfer.com gives you
a safe, fun way to find
more information.

1. Go to www.factsurfer.com.

2. Enter "Australian cattle dogs" into the search box.

3. Click the "Surf" button and select your
   book cover to see a list of related web sites.

Index

The images in this book are reproduced through the courtesy of: Dora Zett, front cover, p. 9 (left); Best dog photo, p. 4; adogslifephoto, p. 5; verschluss, p. 6; everydoghasastory, p. 7; Iryna Dobrovynska, pp. 8-9, 10; Susan Schmitz, p. 9 (right); bgsmith, pp. 11, 13, 16, 17; Aneta Jungerova, p. 12; Csanad Kiss, p. 14; MarkHatfield, p. 15; Tierfotoagentur/ Alamy, pp. 18-19; herreid, p. 19; thka, p. 20; kreinick, p. 21.